COME OUT OF THE VALLEY!

Kenneth Hagin Jr.

Unless otherwise indicated, all Scripture quotations in this volume are from the *King James Version* of the Bible.

Second Printing 1995

ISBN 0-89276-729-4

In the U.S. write:
Kenneth Hagin Ministries
P.O. Box 50126
Tulsa, OK 74150-0126

In Canada write:
Kenneth Hagin Ministries
P.O. Box 335, Station D,
Etobicoke (Toronto), Ontario
Canada, M9A 4X3

Contents

Chapter 1
The Valleys of Sin
And Past Mistakes

It's a beautiful sight to stand on a mountaintop and look down into a valley below. But it's a different perspective altogether when you're in that dark valley trying to get up to the mountaintop above!

We probably all know what it is to go through "valley experiences" or times of trouble and hardship in our lives. But it *is* possible to get out of those valleys. God wants us to continually live on the mountaintop of His victory in Jesus Christ!

You have to come out of your valley if you're going to experience the abundant life God intends for you to have. God has provided the way for you to come out of the valley, but He's not going to do it *for* you.

You have to get yourself out of your valley experiences by coming in line with God's Word. Then you have to make confessions based on what God's Word has to say about your situation.

The first valley we must come out of so we can get in a position to receive from God is *the valley of sin.* That's the valley where we all lived until we realized that we had sinned and come short of the glory of God and then did something about it according to the Word.

How did any of us extract ourselves from that valley

of sin? By getting up one morning and deciding we'd
make a new start? No, we came out of the valley of sin
by realizing our sinful condition and by receiving Jesus
as our Savior.

The valley of sin is the place *every* person will dwell
until they fulfill Romans 10:9: *"That if thou shalt CON-
FESS WITH THY MOUTH THE LORD JESUS, and
shalt BELIEVE IN THINE HEART that God hath
raised him from the dead, thou shalt be saved."*

A lot of people tramped around in the valley of sin
for a long time before they finally discovered how to
climb out and get born again. They didn't like being
bogged down in the mire of sin, but they couldn't find a
way out. They couldn't find a mountain pass — a way to
climb out of that valley.

They got tired of scaling the same steep heights,
only to fall back down into that valley and fail over and
over again. They'd purpose in their hearts not to com-
mit those sins that had kept them bound for so long.
And they'd try again and again to climb up the mountain by the strength of their own willpower.

But they'd only get a little way up the mountain
when the ledge they were standing on would break
from underneath them. And they'd go crashing right
back down again into the midst of all the muck and
mire and degradation of sin. Try as they might, in their
own strength they couldn't get themselves out of the
valley of sin.

Finally, they heard about what Jesus had done for
them on the Cross of Calvary. And they took God at His

Word and voiced their faith with their mouth: "Jesus, I believe You are the Son of God. I believe that in my heart, so I confess it with my mouth."

What happened when those people finally got in line with God's Word and did what Romans 10:9 and 10 says? All of a sudden the mountain became easy to climb. They found the way out of their valley. They were able to climb out of the valley of sin and walk with God onto the mountaintop of a new life in Christ!

Oh, what a beautiful, fertile land lay before them on the other side of the mountain! They just stood in awe on the mountaintop, drinking in the beautiful view of all that God had for them.

They were so used to being trapped and bogged down in the mire. They had hardly seen the sun shine at all in the valley of sin. But now they stood on the mountaintop, looking at all the beautiful blessings that God had provided for them.

But those blessings had been available to them all the time. They just didn't know how to get out of the valley of sin, so they could enjoy God's abundant life.

Other people in the valley of sin realize their sinful condition, but they're not willing to do anything about getting out of that valley. And until they're willing to do something about their condition, no one else can help them.

I often talk to people like that. They tell me, "Oh, I know God is real. And I do want to be a better person." Yet they just keep living the same old way. They're not willing to change.

We may want to reach down and grab ahold of people who are lost in the valley of sin to pull them out of that dark place. But until they are ready to repent of their sin and confess Jesus as their Savior, no one can make them come of that valley — not even God Himself!

Someone may say, "Well, that's a negative statement to make." But, you see, in one sense God has already delivered every person on the face of this earth. God has already said, "I have sent My Son, Jesus. He has shed His blood and redeemed you so you can be free."

But even though God has provided salvation for everyone, each person has to believe in his heart and confess with his mouth that Jesus Christ is his Lord and Savior. That's the *only* way to come out of the valley of sin!

Climb Out of
The Valley of Past Mistakes!

When we come out of the valley of sin, that isn't the stopping point. That's only the beginning! Yes, you begin walking with Jesus as soon as you're born again. But the enemy — the one who bogged you down in the valley of sin — isn't going to quit that easy.

Satan will try to throw obstacles and problems at you to see if he can get you trapped in another valley. For example, if he can't keep you imprisoned in the valley of sin, he'll try to defeat you by putting you in *the valley of past mistakes*. He'll try to bog you down in guilt and condemnation.

But you have to come out of *that* dark valley too. No matter how tough it may seem to be to let go of the past, you have to do it if you want to live on the mountaintop of God's victory.

For example, look at the Apostle Paul. He had to forget a lot of past mistakes. Paul was one of the main instigators of Stephen's stoning. Paul, then known as Saul of Tarsus, had many Christians put to death and cast many others into dungeons as he persecuted the Church of the Lord Jesus Christ.

But then Paul was born again, and God called him to be an apostle to the Gentiles. I'm sure the devil tried to bring memories of Paul's past to his mind to torment him.

But Paul knew he had to forget his past. He knew he had to get out of the valley of past mistakes through his faith in the Lord Jesus Christ. He said, "*...this one thing I do, forgetting those things which are behind, and reaching forth unto those things which are before, I press toward the mark for the prize of the high calling of God in Christ Jesus*" (Phil. 3:13,14).

We can come out of the valley of our past mistakes and past sins too. If we've asked God to forgive us for past sins, we can be assured that God will never remember those sins against us again. That's what the Bible promises us!

MICAH 7:18,19
18 Who is a God like unto thee, THAT PAR-DONETH INIQUITY, and passeth by the transgression of the remnant of his heritage? he retaineth

**not his anger for ever, because he delighteth in
mercy.
19 He will turn again, he will have compassion
upon us; he will subdue our iniquities; and THOU
WILT CAST ALL THEIR SINS INTO THE DEPTHS
OF THE SEA.**

**PSALM 103:12
12 As far as the east is from the west, SO FAR
HATH HE [GOD] REMOVED OUR TRANSGRES-
SIONS FROM US.**

So ask God to forgive you, and then forget the past!
Confess the Word that says, *"There is therefore now NO
CONDEMNATION to them which are in Christ Jesus,
who walk not after the flesh, but after the Spirit"* (Rom.
8:1).

Refuse to live in guilt and condemnation, and go on
down the road of life. Don't remain in that valley of past
mistakes any longer. And never let the devil pull you
back down into that valley of past mistakes again!

Chapter 2
The Valley
Of Financial Despair

Another valley you must come out of is *the valley of financial despair*. That's a valley most of us have walked in at one time or another. Sometimes it can seem like we're walking knee-deep in the mud of that valley!

Many Christians make the mistake of thinking that humility means living in poverty. They think they're being humble by staying in the valley of financial despair.

Yes, we're supposed to be humble. But nowhere in the Word of God does it say that a man is any more spiritual because he lives on Barely-Get-Along Street!

Nowhere does it says he's more righteous because he wears threadbare clothes, shoes stuffed with cardboard to keep the dirt out, and a hat that looks like a dog has chewed it!

That's the way some people read the Word. They think a real spiritual, humble person should live like that. But that's not what the Word of God teaches at all.

Someone may say, "Yes, but the Bible says that money is the root of all evil."

No, that's *not* what the Bible says. The Bible says that the *love of money* is the root of all evil (1 Tim. 6:10).

You might not have one red cent and still love money. You might be as broke as Uncle Jones' old bluetick hound dog lying under the porch and still love money. That's the truth!

You can come out of the valley of financial despair unto the mountaintop of prosperity simply by getting in line with the Word of God. Find out what the Word says about prosperity. Then believe what it says and continually confess what the Word says about your situation.

For instance, Philippians 4:19 says, "*. . . my God SHALL supply all your need according to his riches in glory. . . .*" Someone may say, "Oh, I know, Brother Ken. God will supply our need. Someway, somehow, someday, we'll make it."

But that scripture doesn't say God will just barely help you scrape by! It says God will supply all your needs according to *His riches in glory*. That means He wants to give you an *abundant* supply — *more* than enough!

God promises to abundantly supply our every need. But a lot of people sit in their big easy chair, prop their feet up, lean back, and say, "I'm going to live by faith! Thank You for meeting my needs, Lord." Then they wait for an armored truck full of money to back up and dump it at their door!

But that armored truck isn't coming. God isn't going to supply people's needs when they aren't doing what He's told them to do in His Word.

You see, God didn't say that He'd prosper whatever you *thought about*. He didn't say He would prosper whatever you *desired*. He said He would prosper whatever you *put your hand to* (Deut. 28:8).

Paul, the same man who said that God will supply all your needs according to His riches in glory, also said, "If you don't work, you don't eat" (2 Thess. 3:10).

Then there are some people who think, *I'm going to be a preacher, so I don't have to work.* So they sit around waiting for an opportunity to preach, and they sink into the valley of financial despair.

But if you think the ministry doesn't require work, you'd better change your occupation in a hurry! A true preacher must be ready to work 24 hours a day, 365 days a year. At least when you work a regular eight-hour job, you can go home at night and forget about it until you go back to work the next day!

If you're called to minister the gospel, that's great! But when you first get started in the ministry, you sometimes have to work a secular job *and* do the work of the ministry at the same time.

So preach when you have the opportunity. But work in between preaching engagements if necessary so you can provide for your family. The Bible says to ". . . *Provide things honest in the sight of all men*" (Rom. 12:17).

You see, no matter who you are, *you've* got to do something to get yourself out of the valley of financial despair. You can't just sit around and say, "God's going to meet my needs" when the bills are overdue and there's no food in the house! The Bible says that if you don't provide for your own, you're worse than an infidel (1 Tim. 5:8). That's pretty bad company to be in!

If you'll study the Word of God, you'll find out that the children of Israel had to do whatever God told them to do before they could be blessed. And if they didn't obey God, they didn't receive His blessings.

For instance, God told the Israelites that in order for the death angel to pass over their firstborn children, *they* had to do something. They had to put the blood of a lamb on the doorposts and eat the Passover meal just as He instructed (Exod. 12:1-11).

And when the Israelites were in the wilderness, the Lord said to them, "Gather up manna every day to eat. Don't try to store any because it will spoil" (Exod. 16:16,19).

Then God told the Israelites how much manna to gather for the Sabbath. They could only gather extra for the Sabbath because manna didn't fall on the Sabbath.

God took care of the Israelites in fine fashion as long as they did what He told them to do. God will supply *your* needs, too, as long as you walk by faith and obey His Word.

If you're not getting your needs supplied and you feel like you're bogged down in the mire of poverty and lack, check up on yourself and see if you're slack in obeying God. Make sure you're doing everything God has told you to do. Get in line with God's Word in every area of your life!

Then believe in your heart and confess with your mouth what God's Word says about prosperity. That's the way to come out of the valley of financial despair!

Chapter 3
The Valley of Sickness

One of the devil's favorite strategies against us is to try to put us in *the valley of sickness.* But we have to come out of that dark valley too!

Did you ever stop to ask yourself, *When does the enemy come on the strongest in my life?* Usually Satan likes to hit you the hardest with temptations and problems when you're not feeling well physically. He knows if he can get you down *physically*, it's easier to get you down *spiritually.* That's the truth!

So we must learn how to come out of the valley of sickness. Many people say, "God brought this sickness on me to teach me a lesson." But if sickness is the way God teaches His children lessons, I don't want anything to do with that kind of a Father!

As an earthly father, it hurts me when my children are sick. I'm sure that's true with most parents. Yet people claim that our Heavenly Father teaches His children lessons by putting cancer or some other horrible disease on them!

For instance, I was preaching once in a Florida crusade, and I ministered to a young girl sitting in a wheelchair who had been in an accident.

This girl told me, "I believe I'm in this wheel chair because my family won't submit to God. The Lord put me in this wheelchair so they would turn to Him."

I said, "Young lady, let me set you straight on something. If your relatives think *God* crippled you, then if anything, your being in this wheelchair would cause them to *turn* from God! Who would want to serve a God who cripples His children?

"But," I said, "if you'll get ahold of the Word of God, you can walk out of that chair and go home shouting praises to God's glory. *Then* you'll see your family turn to God! They'll *know* God has performed a miracle for you. They'll say, 'That's the kind of God I want to serve — a God of *power!*' "

It seems strange to me that people can talk about how good and loving God is until they get to the subject of sickness and disease. Then suddenly God changes from a good God to a bad God who puts sickness on people because He wants them to learn something!

But that's not scriptural. God can't get any glory out of someone being pressed down in despair in the valley of sickness.

To come out of the valley of sickness, we must find out what *God's Word* says about healing. We must realize it is God's *will* to heal us (1 Peter 2:24). And we must appropriate His healing power for ourselves.

God is interested in setting His children free, *not* in watching them suffer in the valley of sickness. He wants them to enjoy the mountaintop experience of living a joyous and healthy life.

Sickness and disease robs children of their fathers and mothers. It robs families of much-needed money. Sickness robs, kills, and destroys. And the Bible tells me that anything that robs, kills, and destroys is of the devil (John 10:10). It has nothing to do with God!

God didn't send His Son, Jesus Christ, to destroy people. No, He sent Jesus to destroy the works of the *devil* (1 John 3:8). God sent His Son to seek and to save the lost (Luke 19:10). And He sent Jesus to deliver us and set us free from sickness, despondency, and despair.

So we must believe and confess what God says. First Peter 2:24 says, ". . . *by whose stripes ye were healed.*" That's simple. Why can't we just believe that and walk out of the valley of sickness?

One Woman Who Climbed Out Of Her Valley of Sickness

There *is* a way to walk out of the valley of sickness. In Mark chapter 5, we find the account of the woman with the issue of blood. She discovered the way to come out of her valley of sickness.

> **MARK 5:25-29**
> **25 And a certain woman, which had an issue of blood twelve years,**
> **26 And had suffered many things of many physicians, and had spent all that she had, and was nothing bettered, but rather grew worse,**
> **27 When she had HEARD OF JESUS, CAME in the press behind, and TOUCHED his garment.**
> **28 For she SAID, If I may touch but his clothes, I SHALL BE WHOLE.**
> **29 And straightway the fountain of her blood was dried up; and she felt in her body that SHE WAS HEALED OF THAT PLAGUE.**

This woman was sick with an incurable blood condition. We know from the Word that the life is in the blood (Lev. 17:11). Therefore, that incurable blood disease was gradually sapping the life out of this woman.

Every day she felt a little weaker. Every day she found herself with a little less strength and willpower to fight for life. It had been a long fight for this woman. She had been fighting this incurable blood disease for twelve years!

The Bible says this woman spent all she had on physicians. That seems to indicate she'd spent quite a lot of money on doctors trying to get well. She may have been quite wealthy when she first got sick.

She'd been to many doctors and had spent all of her money. But after all that, she wasn't any better than she was when she went to the first doctor.

She got the same bad report from every doctor she went to. Each doctor did all he knew to do, and each one gave her the same verdict: "I'm sorry. We can't help you."

Then this woman heard about Jesus! She said, "I know what I'll do. I've tried everything else to extract myself out of this valley of sickness I'm living in. I'll go to Jesus!"

This woman didn't sit and wait for Jesus to come to *her*. She got up and went to *Jesus*.

If *you're* going to get out of the valley of sickness, you can't sit down and wait around for your healing. You've got to get up and do something yourself.

What should you do? Go to where Jesus is. He's up

on the mountaintop of victory, so get up and climb the mountain! Get up into the clouds of glory and enjoy the beauty of the mountaintop. Look back down into the valley of sickness and say, "Look what Jesus has delivered me from!"

That's what this woman did. She went to Jesus, despite the fact that she lived in a day when it wasn't acceptable for a woman to be out mixing in public. Not only that, but according to Jewish Law, people with incurable diseases were supposed to keep away from other folks because they were unclean.

But this woman didn't let any of these obstacles hinder her. She just said, "I've heard of Jesus, and I'm going to find Him! If I can only touch His clothes, I know I'll be whole!" So she went and touched Jesus, and something supernatural happened!

Friend, you cannot go to Jesus and touch Him in faith without something wonderful happening. Jesus is ever ready and always present to minister to you. But He only ministers to you as *you* come to *Him*.

Read the Bible. You'll find that throughout the Word of God — starting with salvation and including every other blessing you receive from God — it's as you come to the Lord that He ministers to you. It's *not* as you sit down and moan, "Well, here I am, Lord. I'm waiting for You to come and give me what I need."

Many people want someone else to pray and receive their healing for them. But God wants His children to learn how to receive what they need from Him on their *own* faith.

No one else has to go to God for you — you can come to Him yourself!

If you want to extract yourself from the valley of sickness, you must come to Jesus *yourself*. Don't depend on someone else to do it for you. *You* must come to Jesus with *your* faith.

Someone else can agree in prayer with you, but he can't get your answer for you. If you're going to climb up to the mountaintop and enjoy the sunlight of God's healing power, you'll have to do something yourself!

Before the woman with the issue of blood found Jesus, she was in her darkest hour. For twelve years she had fought this sickness. The Bible says that she spent all she had. She couldn't go to one more doctor, because she didn't have any more money. It seemed that she had no hope whatsoever.

But then this woman heard about a Man by the Name of Jesus. She heard that you didn't need any money to come to this Man. It didn't matter whether you had a million dollars or no money at all.

This Man just said, "All you who are weary and heavy laden, come unto Me. My yoke is easy and My burden is light" (Matt. 11:28,30).

Friend, Jesus is still the same today as He was yesterday. And He's still saying, "Come unto Me. You don't have to buy what you need from Me. I'll freely give you whatever you need."

You don't need money to receive what you need from God. All you need is faith in what God has said. All you need to do is believe God's Word. It doesn't cost you a thing.

If we had to buy the answers to our prayers, none of us would ever receive anything. None of us has enough money to purchase eternal life. But, thank God, all we have to do is believe in Jesus Christ as our Savior, and He freely gives us eternal life!

This woman in Mark 5 had never heard a faith lesson in her life. All she had heard was that a Man by the Name of Jesus went about doing good, healing all who were sick and oppressed.

She heard He was anointed by the power of God and that this healing power was free. And when this woman heard about Jesus, she said, "I'm going to Jesus. If I can touch His clothes, I'll be whole."

So this woman gathered all her strength and found the crowd that followed Jesus. She was determined to get to Jesus, no matter how hard it would be to push through that crowd.

I've been in a situation where a crowd of people were walking all crammed together down a dusty road, and there was someone in the middle of the crowd that all those people wanted to see.

It's hard to see what's going on in that kind of situation. The dust swirls, and the crowds shove and push each other. All those people crammed together keep you from getting closer to the one who's the center of attraction, because everyone else is desperately trying to get closer too.

I can imagine that this woman encountered a similar situation. But she didn't let the dust and the crowds deter her at all. She started pressing through that crowd. She wriggled through one gap in the crowd, and then she pressed through another. She just kept trying to get through that crowd to reach Jesus.

In all her effort to get to Jesus, that woman probably started feeling weak. I'm sure the enemy was trying to get her discouraged so she'd give up.

The devil probably told her: "You're never going to make it! You might as well give up. And even if you do get to Jesus, nothing's going to happen. It's all a hoax! Someone just made it all up. There's nothing to this healing business!"

However, despite the devil's attempts to discourage this woman with the issue of blood, she kept on pressing through the crowd until she reached Jesus.

She believed in Jesus' ability to heal her, so with the one last bit of strength in her body, she reached out and touched His garment in faith. When she did that, something supernatural happened! She was completely healed! Jesus turned to her and said, "Daughter, thy faith has made thee whole."

The Bible says that *virtue* went out of Jesus (Mark 5:30). That word "virtue" is "dunamis" in the Greek, and it means *power*. It's the same word we get the word "dynamite" from.

So the power that went out of Jesus when this woman touched Him was a dynamite kind of power. Now that's a lot of power! And that mighty dunamis power did something supernatural. It made that woman *whole*!

Jesus turned around and said, "Who touched me?" Impetuous Peter said, "Who touched You? What are You talking about, Lord? Look at this crowd! They're all reaching out to touch You, and yet You ask, 'Who touched me?'"

But Jesus said, "No, someone touched me *in faith*, and power went out of me."

You see, you can be around Jesus all the time, but if you never touch Him with the touch of faith, the power's not going to come forth from Him to meet your need. You have to *expect* that your need will be met and touch Him in faith!

Notice that nothing happened when other people just casually bumped against Jesus or touched him out of curiosity. Those people stayed in the same valley they were in before they touched Him.

But this woman who had faith said, "If I can touch Him, something *will* happen. I *will* be made whole." And when she touched Him, she received exactly what she came for. She came out of her valley of sickness!

Why was she made completely whole? Because she spent the only thing she had left — faith in what she'd heard about Jesus. She believed that Jesus would make her whole, and then she acted on her faith.

That's how the woman with the issue of blood came out of the valley of sickness. And that's the way *you* can come out of that valley too!

Chapter 4
Blast Your Way Out
Of Your Valleys!

The woman with issue of blood blasted her way out of the valley of sickness by receiving the *dunamis* or *power* of God by faith. She didn't know it, but she was using the same faith principles that Jesus gave us in Mark 11:23.

In this scripture, Jesus taught us how to activate God's power to blast away obstacles so we can walk out of any valley the enemy tries to put us in.

> **MARK 11:23**
> **23 For verily I say unto you, That whosoever shall SAY unto this mountain, Be thou removed, and be thou cast into the sea; and shall not doubt in his heart, but SHALL BELIEVE that those things which he SAITH shall come to pass; he SHALL HAVE whatsoever he SAITH.**

The law of faith Jesus is talking about here is to believe in your heart what God says, confess it with your mouth, and then act on what you believe. Let's see exactly how the woman with the issue of blood obeyed this spiritual law.

What did this woman do when she heard about Jesus? She *said*, "I know what I'll do. I'll go to Jesus and touch the hem of His garment. And when I touch Jesus, I'm going to receive my healing!" She *said* it!

First, she *believed* in her heart that Jesus could heal her. Second, she *said* it with her mouth. Third, she *did* something about it. She went to Jesus and touched the hem of His garment in faith. And then she *received* what she had said was hers! That's exactly what Jesus said to do in Mark 11:23!

The Bible says, *"Faith cometh by hearing, and hearing by the Word of God"* (Rom. 10:17). Jesus is the *living* Word (John 1:1). So when this woman heard about Jesus, faith came to her.

In the same way, when we read or listen to the written Word, faith comes to us. That's the only way we can make our faith grow. We don't get more faith by praying for it.

The Bible says God has given every person the measure of faith (Rom. 12:3). We don't have to *get* any more faith. We just need to *use* and *develop* the faith we already have!

It was by the measure of faith God gave you that you received salvation. You use that same measure of faith to receive every other blessing that's promised in the Word.

Faith in God's Word is like a blasting cap to a stick of dynamite. If you throw a stick of dynamite down on the ground and it doesn't have a blasting cap on it, nothing will happen. But once you put a blasting cap on that stick of dynamite, watch out! If you throw it down and that blasting cap hits just right, that dynamite will ignite and explode!

In the same way, when you use the measure of faith according to Mark 11:23, it becomes a blasting cap to the dynamite power of God. Just add that blasting cap of faith to God's power. It will blast you out of any valley the enemy tries to trap you in!

What happens if you hook up a bundle of dynamite to a detonator, put the dynamite on a mountainside, and set off the charge? The blasting caps will ignite, and the explosion will blow a huge hole in that mountain!

That natural example of dynamite can help you understand how to operate the spiritual law of faith. The power of God, which is like the power of a dynamite blast, is available to us. We just have to ignite it with our faith. We do that by believing God's Word in our hearts and confessing it with our mouths.

You *can* come out of any valley you may be in right now by blasting your way out with God's Word! There's no use for you to wallow in the muck and mire of sin, condemnation, poverty, or sickness! There's a way out of that mess!

I don't care if the devil has thrown all kinds of obstacles in the path that leads out of the valley. Jesus already told you in Mark 11:23, "Just believe in your heart and say unto any problem or obstacle, "Get out of my way!" and it will be removed." That's the way to blast those obstacles out of your way, so you can come out of *any* valley!

It's Your Choice!

There are so many people who think they need to stay in their valley because *God* has put them there.

They think God is a mean old Ruler sitting up in Heaven looking down on the earth with a giant fly swatter in His hand, just looking for someone to hit. And every time someone does something wrong, He swats them and says, "Ha! I got you, Buddy!"

That's the way a lot of people picture God. But God's not that way at all!

The *enemy* is the one who's mean! It's the enemy who tries to entangle us in his snares and bog us down in his valleys of defeat. It's the devil who tries to overwhelm us with storms from every side. He likes to trap us down in the shadows where we can't even see the daylight because the mountains are so high.

The devil will keep you captive down in his valleys of defeat as long as you let him. You see, it's your choice. You can choose to continue to walk in those valley experiences of trial and temptation. In fact, you can live in the valley all your life and still be born again, filled with the Spirit, and Heaven-bound.

But I want to tell you something. God doesn't want you to live in the valley of defeat. He wants you to act on His Word in faith, blast your way out of the valley, and live an abundant life in Jesus!

Living for Jesus is the greatest life there is! God doesn't intend for us to lack in *any* area of our lives — spiritual, physical, or financial. He has made provision to meet our every need in His Word. He wants us to live on the mountaintop of victory *all* the time!

Are you in a dark valley right now? Are you thinking, *I'd sure like to see the sun for a change?*

Well, take the Word of God and blast your way out of it! Then climb up to the mountaintop where the sun shines and the rivers flow freely. Walk in freedom where the birds sing and the cool breeze blows. Get out of that valley! You *can* do it with God's Word!

There's some of you who have been in the valley so long, you may think you need someone to help get you out. But if you'll take the same faith principles that the woman with the issue of blood used, you can come out of that valley yourself! Jesus said to that woman, *"Thy faith* has made thee whole."

Someone might argue, "Yes, but it was easy for that woman to receive her miracle. She could go straight to *Jesus.* But He's not on earth anymore! I can't go to Him like she did."

But you don't need Jesus here in person so you can touch the hem of His garment. The power of God is inside of *you* because the Holy Spirit dwells within you!

You see, when Jesus was here on earth, everyone had to go to Him to receive God's power. At that time, Jesus was the only person on earth who was full of the Holy Spirit and power.

His disciples had some of God's power operating in their lives during Jesus' earthly ministry, but they didn't operate in it consistently. For instance, several times, the disciples came to Him with someone in need and said, "We couldn't help him, Master."

But then later on Jesus Christ became the supreme Sacrifice on the Cross. He rose again and ascended to Heaven to sit down at the Father's right hand. And the

Father said, "All right, Holy Spirit, go down to the earth and empower My people. It's the Day of Pentecost, and there are 120 people down there in that Upper Room waiting for You."

On that Day of Pentecost in the Upper Room, the same Holy Spirit who anointed Jesus with God's power, also filled and empowered those 120 believers.

Today you and I are recipients of the same mighty power that Jesus was anointed with — the power of the Holy Spirit. But the Holy Spirit hasn't just anointed us on the outside; He also dwells *inside* of us because we're born again.

In the Book of John, Jesus predicted that the Holy Spirit would dwell in us like a well of water and cause rivers of living water to flow from our innermost being (John 4:14; 7:37). Jesus didn't say just one river would flow out of us. He said *rivers* of living water would flow from us.

God's power is always available to us as believers. We can draw upon those rivers of living water inside us — the mighty power of the Holy Spirit — to blast our way out of our valleys.

We can also take God's power to the person who doesn't know how to get out of his valley. We can tell him, "Let me show you how to blast those obstacles out of your way. Let me help you climb out of that dark valley!"

The power of God is just as real today as it was when Jesus walked on the earth. And in these last days before Jesus returns, God is raising up a new breed of people. He's raising up a mighty army of believers to face the onslaughts of the enemy.

In the days ahead, we will face obstacles that are greater than any of us can imagine right now. And with God's wisdom and grace, we'll blast through every one of those obstacles with the mighty power of God!

You see, Jesus Christ is not coming for a defeated Church. He's not coming for a defeated Bride. The Word says He's coming for a powerful Church — a spotless Bride who has overcome the enemy's strategies (Rev. 3:5).

Jesus is coming for a Body of believers who have blasted their obstacles out of their way by the power of God so they can climb high onto the mountaintop of victory. *That's* the kind of Church Jesus is coming for!

Someone may say, "Yes, but, Brother Ken, you just don't know what I've got to face in life."

The Word of God doesn't say that faith in God will work except in difficult cases. It says that you have authority in Jesus' Name over *all* the power of the enemy (Luke 10:19)! You can come out of any valley if you will dare to believe and act on God's Word!

We all face valley experiences in life. But it's up to each of us whether we remain in the valley or climb up to the mountaintop of God's abundant life.

As you face the valleys in your life, remember that God is still with you. The enemy will try to make you think that God has forgotten all about you. But God *never* leaves you, nor forsakes you (Heb. 13:5). So turn to the Lord. He's the One who can help you.

The devil may try to put you in dark valley experiences. But you can walk through those valleys with the Lord at your side. You can come out on the other side shouting the victory. Then you can say just as the Apostle Paul said, "I thank my God I *always* triumph in Christ Jesus" (2 Cor. 2:14)!

Are you ready to come out of your valley? Friend, it's up to you. You must make your decision to come out of all the muck and mire that has bogged you down in life. No one else can make that decision for you — not your spouse, your parents, your friends, or your pastor.

No one can extract you out of your valley but *you*. Of course, you can't deliver yourself out of your valley in your own strength. But, thank God, through Jesus Christ and His Word, you have the power to come out of *any* valley!

So make this decision: "I will *not* let the enemy lord it over me and keep me in the valley. I shall come out of this valley. I will ascend to the mountain summit, and I will bask in the glow of the Son of God Himself!"